Astronomy Now!™

A Look at
MERCURY

Mary R. Dunn

PowerKiDS
press
New York

Dedicated to my husband, Michael

Published in 2008 by The Rosen Publishing Group, Inc.
29 East 21st Street, New York, NY 10010

First Edition

Editor: Amelie von Zumbusch
Book Design: Greg Tucker
Photo Researcher: Nicole Pristash

Photo Credits: Cover © William Radcliffe/Getty Images; pp. 5, 19, 21 Courtesy NASA/JPL-Caltech; p. 7 © Shutterstock.com; pp. 7 (inset), 15 Courtesy NASA; pp. 9, 12 (top and bottom), p. 13 (top and bottom), p. 17 (main and inset) © Getty Images; p. 11 © PhotoDisc.

Library of Congress Cataloging-in-Publication Data

Dunn, Mary R.
  A look at Mercury / Mary R. Dunn. — 1st ed.
      p. cm. — (Astronomy now)
  Includes index.
  ISBN-13: 978-1-4042-3825-1 (library binding)
  ISBN-10: 1-4042-3825-5 (library binding)
  1. Mercury (Planet)—Juvenile literature. I. Title.
  QB611.D86 2008
  523.41—dc22

                                            2007001052

Manufactured in the United States of America

Contents

The Planet Mercury

Mercury is a small, gray **planet** in our **solar system**. Unlike the other planets in our solar system, Mercury has no moon. Mercury is the planet closest to the Sun. This makes it hard to see.

People long ago discovered Mercury. Thousands of years ago, the Greeks watched the heavens and saw what they called traveling stars. Some of these stars seemed to appear just in the morning or at night. The Greeks called one of the morning stars Apollo. They called one of the evening stars Hermes. We now know that both of these traveling stars were the planet Mercury.

Mercury is a very small planet. The planets Jupiter and Saturn both have moons that are larger than Mercury!

5

Mercury's Orbit

Planets move around the Sun in paths called orbits. Mercury travels around the Sun in its orbit more quickly than any other planet. It takes Earth 365 days, or one year, to go around the Sun. Mercury orbits the Sun in just 88 days. Therefore, one year on Mercury lasts 88 days.

Mercury races around the Sun in an elliptical, or egg-shaped, orbit. This means that Mercury is sometimes as close as 28 million miles (45 million km) to the Sun. At other times, it is as far as 43 million miles (69 million km) away from the Sun.

This picture shows the order of the planets orbiting our Sun. *Inset:* Mercury is the closest planet to the Sun.

Mercury's Axis

As Mercury travels along its orbit, it spins slowly on its axis. An axis is a pretend line through the center of a planet. As Mercury spins, half of the planet faces the Sun. It is day on that side of the planet. It is night on the other side. A day on Mercury lasts about as long as 59 days on Earth.

Mercury has only a thin **atmosphere** to guard it from the Sun. Therefore, days on Mercury can be as hot as 800° F (427° C). At night, Mercury can be as cold as -280° F (-173° C).

The side of Mercury
you see in this picture
is the side where it is
day. The part of the
planet where it is night
is hidden in darkness.

9

The Smallest Planet

Mercury is our solar system's smallest planet. **Astronomers** think Mercury is made of iron on the inside and rock on the outside. Mercury has a lot of iron for such a small planet. Astronomers believe the iron inside Mercury causes its **magnetic field**. Mercury and Earth are our solar system's only small planets with magnetic fields.

Earth is bigger than Mercury, so Earth's **gravity** is stronger. This means objects weigh more on Earth than they would on Mercury. For example, if an object weighed 50 pounds (23 kg) on Earth, it would weigh about 19 pounds (9 kg) on Mercury.

Here you can see how
much bigger Earth (top)
is than Mercury.

Cool Facts

Mark Twain

Mercury has large, round holes called craters on it. The planet's craters are generally named after well-known artists and writers, like Auguste Renoir and Mark Twain.

Mercury is named for the speedy Roman messenger god who had wings on his shoes.

Mercury

Mercury is 11 times brighter than Earth because it is so close to the Sun.

Mercury now looks much as it did soon after it was formed. It has changed so little that it is called a dead world.

A Mercury Timeline

2004 – Scientists send off *Messenger* to visit Mercury.

1974 – The spacecraft *Mariner 10* takes the first pictures of Mercury.

1631 – Astronomer Pierre Gassendi sees Mercury cross in front of the Sun. This is called a transit of Mercury.

Fun Figures

Mercury travels around the Sun at 8 miles per second (13 km/s).

Though it is the smallest planet, Mercury is still 3,032 miles (4,480 km) wide.

The closest that Mercury gets to Earth is 48 million miles (77 million km) away.

Mercury's Beginning

Mercury formed over four **billion** years ago. At that time, space dust and **hydrogen** gas came together. They formed a big, spinning cloud. As the cloud spun, it gathered more gas and dust.

The cloud spun faster and faster. This made part of the cloud flatten out into a disk, or a flat, round shape. The matter in the middle of the disk grew hot. It came together and formed the star that is our Sun. Pieces of matter from the outside of the disk came together to form objects, too. They became moons and planets, such as Mercury.

This colorful cloud of gas is the Orion Nebula. New stars are forming there. Scientists study nebulas to help them understand the cloud of gas from which our own solar system formed.

The Craters of Mercury

Scientists believe Mercury's **surface** has not changed much since it first formed. The planet looks much like Earth's Moon. It has small mountains. It also has deep holes called craters. These craters were formed by rocks that crashed into Mercury.

Astronomers think that about four billion years ago rocks flew through space like rain. The rocks crashed into planets and formed craters. Some planets, like Earth, have thick atmospheres that burn up some of these rocks before they can form craters. However, Mercury's very thin atmosphere did not slow the rocks down. Therefore, Mercury has lots of craters.

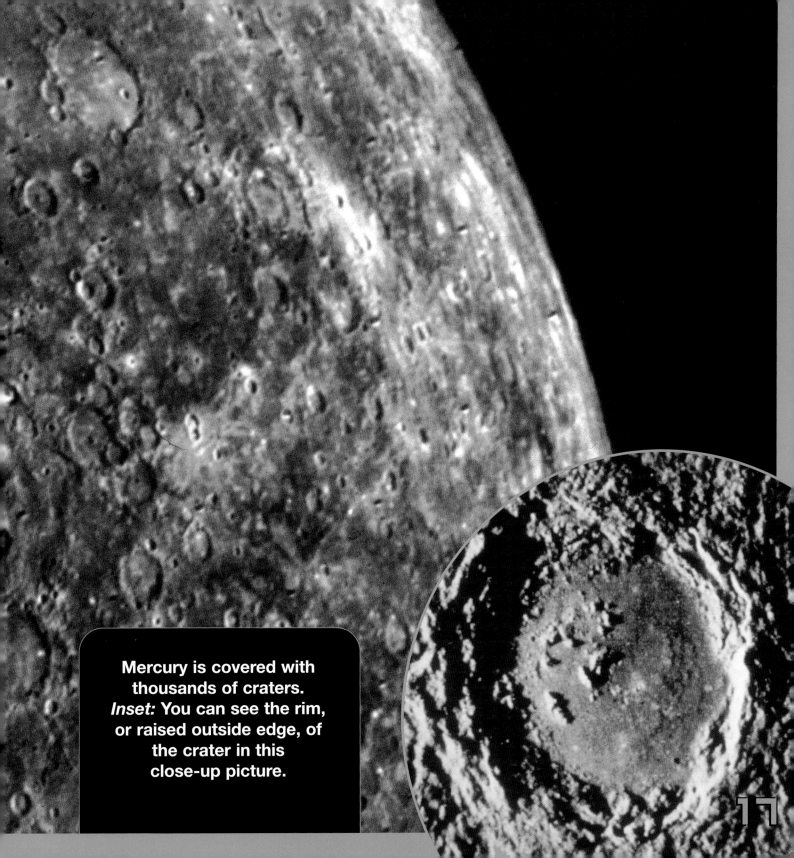

Mercury is covered with
thousands of craters.
Inset: You can see the rim,
or raised outside edge, of
the crater in this
close-up picture.

17

The Caloris Basin

Mercury's biggest crater formed billions of years ago, when a huge rock crashed into the planet and made a big, round crater. Scientists named the crater the Caloris Basin. Large craters are called basins. At about 800 miles (1,287 km) wide, the Caloris Basin is about the size of the state of Texas!

Scientists think that the crash that formed the Caloris Basin caused melted rock called lava to flow from the inside of the planet. The lava filled the crater. When the lava cooled and hardened, it made parts of the crater's floor as flat as an icy pond.

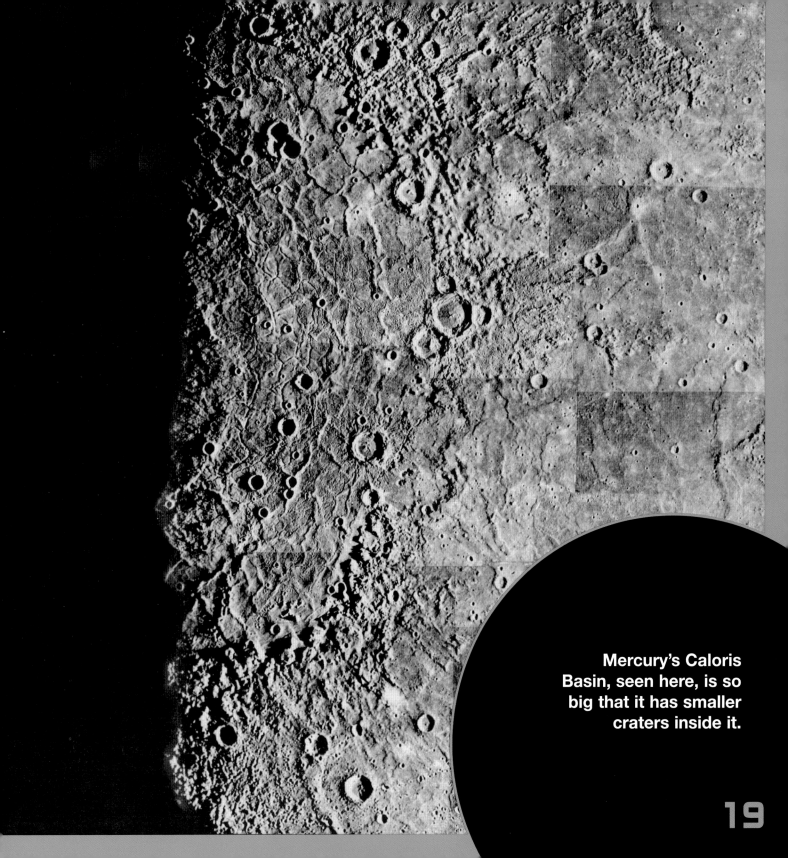

Mercury's Caloris
Basin, seen here, is so
big that it has smaller
craters inside it.

19

Scarps

Along with craters, Mercury has rocky cliffs called scarps. Some scarps are short. Others are nearly 2 miles (3 km) high. Astronomers think Mercury's scarps formed because the planet cooled after it formed. As Mercury cooled, it grew smaller and caved in on itself. This left bits of the planet's surface sticking up as scarps.

The biggest scarp on Mercury is more than 300 miles (482 km) long. Its name is Discovery Rupes. Astronomers name scarps after important ships. Discovery Rupes is named after *Discovery*, which was **explorer** Captain James Cook's ship.

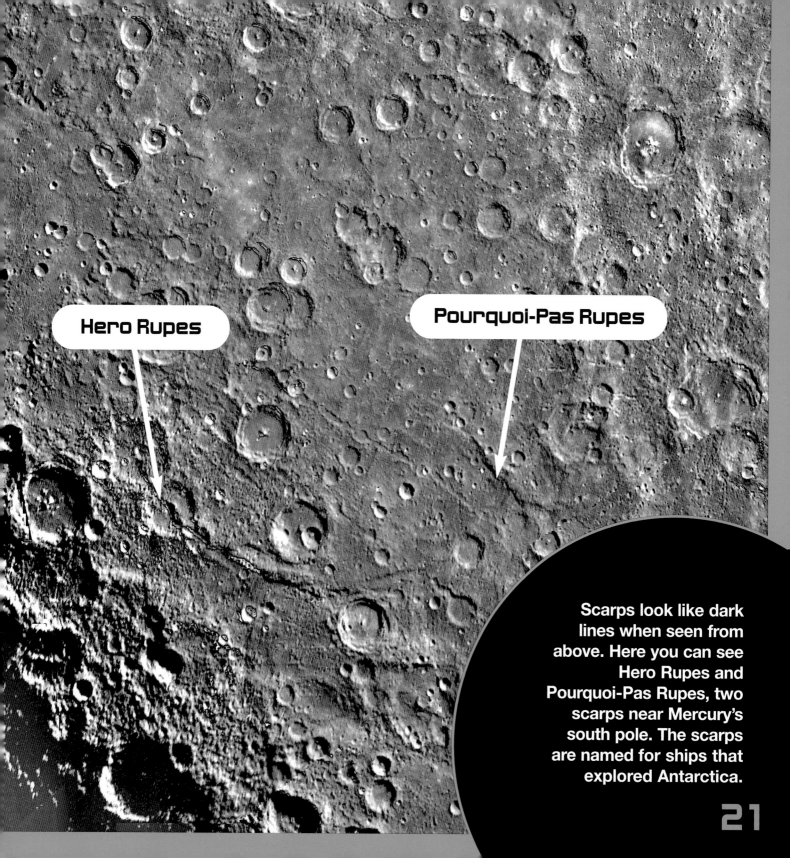

Hero Rupes

Pourquoi-Pas Rupes

Scarps look like dark lines when seen from above. Here you can see Hero Rupes and Pourquoi-Pas Rupes, two scarps near Mercury's south pole. The scarps are named for ships that explored Antarctica.

21

Learning More About Mercury

Scientists still have much to learn about Mercury. In August 2004, they sent off a rocket from Cape Canaveral, Florida, to learn more. The rocket held a space probe, or ship, called *Messenger*.

A few minutes after blast-off, the rocket let go of *Messenger* and the probe began its trip toward Mercury. *Messenger* carries many new tools. It will enter Mercury's orbit in 2011. It will take pictures of Mercury and find out more about the inside of the planet. Scientists hope *Messenger* will teach them not only about Mercury, but also about how our solar system was formed.

Glossary

astronomers (uh-STRAH-nuh-merz) People who study the Sun, the Moon, the planets, and the stars.

atmosphere (AT-muh-sfeer) The layer of gases around an object in space.

billion (BIL-yun) A thousand millions.

explorer (ek-SPLOR-ur) A person who travels and looks for new land.

gravity (GRA-vih-tee) The force that causes objects to move toward each other. The bigger an object is, the more gravity it has.

hydrogen (HY-dreh-jen) A colorless gas that burns easily and weighs less than any other known kind of matter.

magnetic field (mag-NEH-tik FEELD) A strong force made by currents that flow through metals and other matter.

planet (PLA-net) A large object, such as Earth, that moves around the Sun.

scientists (SY-un-tists) People who study the world.

solar system (SOH-ler SIS-tem) A group of planets that circles a star.

surface (SER-fes) The outside of anything.

Index

A

astronomers, 10, 16, 20

atmosphere(s), 8, 16

D

day(s), 6, 8

E

Earth, 6, 8, 10, 16

H

heavens, 4

Hermes, 4

hydrogen, 14

I

inside, 10, 22

iron, 10

M

magnetic field, 10

moon(s), 4, 14

morning, 5

N

night, 4, 8

O

object(s), 10, 14

orbit(s), 6, 8, 22

outside, 10, 14

R

rock(s), 10, 16, 18

S

scientists, 16, 18, 22

shape, 14

solar system, 4, 22

star(s), 4, 14

Sun, 4, 6, 8, 14

surface, 16, 20

Y

year(s), 4, 6, 14, 16, 18

Web Sites

Due to the changing nature of Internet links, PowerKids Press has developed an online list of Web sites related to the subject of this book. This site is updated regularly. Please use this link to access the list: www.powerkidslinks.com/astro/mercury/